Getting Started with the French Knitter Tool

This booklet showcases French knitting, also known as "spool knitting." This form of knitting conjures up childhood memories of a wooden spool with four finishing nails hammered around the core. With this device, you formed a long knitted tube (known as an I-cord). Later, you might coil it into a hot pad. This book takes this basic process, then adds modern assorted beads and an array of fibers to get contemporary French knitting projects—glamorous, spectacular jewelry pieces. I present specific projects here so you can see how the process works. You will be delighted to see how easy it is to create jewelry in your own style.

The French Knitter Tool

I recommend the French Knitter, a bead jewelry tool manufactured by Clover Needlecraft Incorporated. This tool has great versatility. The interchangeable heads each have a different number of pegs. Included also is a hook that allows for easy manipulation of the stitch over the peg. This tool fits comfortably in your hand.

To remove the head, turn the head counterclockwise and gently pull up.

To attach the head, set the head in the notches on the main body and turn clockwise until it clicks.

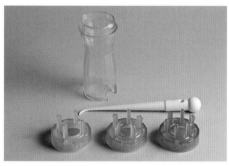

French Knitter tool. Main body, 4-peg head, 5-peg head, 6-peg head, hook.

Fibers & Beads

Fibers

Traditionally, knitters used hemp and yarns with the French Knitter tool. Today there is a growing selection of fibers and fashion colors available to complement any project. In this booklet, we most often use yarn with metallic threads, bead-stringing wire, monofilament, 2-ply lamé cord, Perle cotton, embroidery floss, and leather. No doubt you will establish your own palette of favorite colors and cords.

Tip: Beyond appearances, the "touch" and tensile strength of the fibers are important considerations. If the fiber is hard to work with or breaks frequently, it is best for you to find an alternative.

Fibers. There are many types and colors of fibers to use.

Beads

The array of sizes, colors, and materials in the bead world can be overwhelming! How the French Knitter is used will help you navigate through this maze.

Beads are knit, not strung, into the jewelry. The number of beads used in French knitting is dependent on how many pegs are used and how often beads are added to the knitting.

The width of the bead eyelet must easily pass over the fiber. Good planning is necessary before running off to the bead store. For all of the pieces in this booklet, we use E beads (about 4mm), 6mm, and 8mm.

If you use larger beads (8mm), you must also consider how many can fit down the "throat" of the French knitter. You may also want to use the head with four pegs because it has more space between pegs and less beads in the knitted round. Also, using a larger bead in combination with smaller ones allows for that bead to slide down the throat more easily.

Bead sizes. The Beach Glass Bracelet uses a 4-peg head and all larger beads, while the Silver & Black Bracelet uses the 5-peg head and intermittent large beads.

Tip: Sequins and buttons are great substitutes for beads.

Findings

You'll also need a few types of findings to complete these projects—all the necessary clasps and parts for necklaces, earrings, and other types of jewelry.

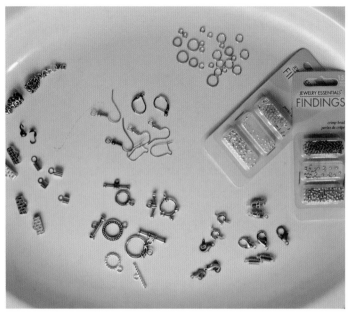

Findings. Jump rings, toggle clasps, earring wires, crimp beads, ribbon clasps, and end caps.

Additional Tools

In addition to the items listed previously, you will need some basic jewelry-making tools to complete the projects found here, such as wire cutters, glue, and wonder clips.

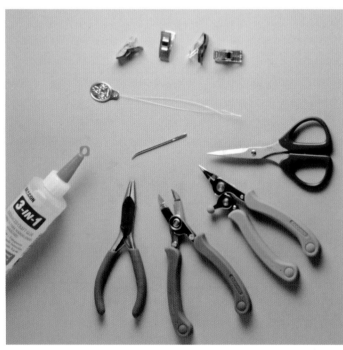

Tools. Bead threader, pliers, wire cutters, scissors, glue, darning needle, and wonder clips.

General Instructions & Methods

Each project makes reference to this section so you can achieve consistency and good results. The two methods described below accomplish the same results. Which you choose is up to you: some people like both techniques; others prefer to focus on only one. There are three heads with peg options. All options use Method A or Method B and can produce a single or double-loop stitch. The differences are noticeable in the tube width and density.

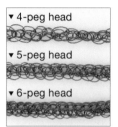

Method A Single Loop.

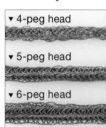

Method A Double Loop.

Method A: Single-Loop Stitch (Knit Over One Row)

1 Pre-string the beads. String beads on fiber before knitting.

2 Insert fiber. Insert fiber from top of center hole of main body and pull through hole. Leave approximately 8" (20cm) of fiber extending from bottom hole; hold fiber firm to the main body while knitting.

3 Make Row 1. Wrap fiber around each peg as illustrated (Row 1).

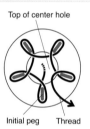

Top of center hole

Initial peg   Thread

4 Make Row 2. Repeat Step 3 to create Row 2. Start adding 1 bead between each peg.

Bead

Row 1

Initial peg   Row 2

5 Knit Row 1. Insert hook into Row 1, pull strand off toward the inside of the peg. This is the knit stitch. Knit all of Row 1 in this manner.

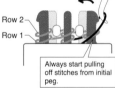

Row 2
Row 1

Always start pulling off stitches from initial peg.

6 Progress. Wrap another row of stitches; then knit off the lowest stitch (Row 2) from each peg as in the previous step. Repeat this process.

Method A: Double-Loop Stitch (Knit Over Two Rows)

1–4 Get started. Steps 1–4 are the same as the single loop method.

5 Make Row 3. Wrap an additional row of fiber around each peg (Row 3).

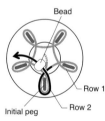

Row 3 bead

Row 2

Row 2 bead

Initial peg   Row 3

6 Knit. Insert hook into Row 1, pull strand off toward the inside of the peg over 2 rows.

7 Progress. Wrap the next row; then knit the stitches of the lowest row. Repeat this process.

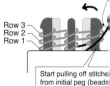

Row 3
Row 2
Row 1

Start pulling off stitches from initial peg (beads not shown here).

Method B: Single-Loop Stitch (Knit Over One Row)

1 Pre-string the beads. String beads on fiber before knitting.

2 Insert fiber. Insert fiber from top of center hole of main body and pull through hole. Leave approximately 8" (20cm) of fiber extending from the main body base; hold fiber arm to main body while knitting.

3 Make Row 1. Wrap fiber around each peg as illustrated (Row 1).

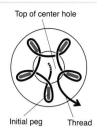

Top of center hole

Initial peg · Thread

4 Wrap the head. Wrap the fiber around the entire head as illustrated (Row 2).

Bead

Initial peg

5 Make the knit stitch. Insert hook into Row 1, pull stitch off toward the inside of the peg. This is the knit stitch. Knit all of Row 1 in this manner.

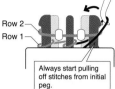

Row 2
Row 1

Always start pulling off stitches from initial peg.

6 Continue. Repeat Steps 4 and 5.

Method B: Double-Loop Stitch (Knit Over Two Rows)

1–4 Get started. Steps 1–4 are the same as the single loop B method.

5 Wrap the head. After Step 4 wrap around the entire head to make one more row.

6 Continue. Pull Row 1 stitches over Rows 2 and 3. Repeat.

Tip: Keep these wraps loose for easy knitting.

Finishing for Method A & B (Casting Off)

1 Cut the fiber. Cut the fiber, leaving approximately an 8" (20cm) tail.

2 Knit off. Wrap fiber around one peg. Insert hook into lower row and knit off the stitch.

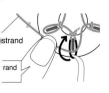

strand

rand

3 Pull out fiber. Pull out fiber wrapped in Step 2 above.

4 Continue. Repeat Steps 2 and 3 on all pegs with the end of the strand and pull lightly.

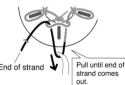

End of strand

Pull until end of strand comes out.

Design Strategies

This section gives you a running start on finishing your piece. Through trial and error, I have learned much that I can share with you. The information in this section will save you time and help avoid common mistakes.

Fiber vs. Beads

Inspiration. I loved this yarn and loved these beads! I thought I'd try using them together.

Undesirable results. Unfortunately, the beads in the yarn all but disappeared due to the quick change in the variegated coloring. This also happens when bead and fiber colors are similar (lower example).

Solution. Because this rainbow yarn is stand-alone beautiful, I knitted without beads (lower necklace). And the beads really are visible against the neutral gold lamé cord (necklace held by model)!

Rachael Porter

Beaded necklace or wrapped bracelet. These necklaces can be worn as a pair or separately.

Bead Placement & Use

Although instructions for the use of the French Knitter call for it, you do not always need to place a bead between every peg on every row! Imagine using the 6-peg head and dropping a bead every round...that's 6, 12, 18, 24 ...24 total beads in just 4 rounds!

Bead options. You have options of adding beads between every other peg, every other row, and many other combinations. This allows more flexibilty with your own designs and helps conserve your supply of beads.

Tailored vs. Chunky Appearance

Appearance really has to do with bead choice, and sometimes fiber. If you use the same size bead throughout construction, you will come up with a consistent and tailored look. If you use beads that are different sizes or irregular shapes, the finished piece will look chunky.

Measurements & Stretch

There are two things to remember when you calculate the length of the finished piece.

1. All things knitted stretch...whether or not you use stretchy cord!
2. If you intend to include a closure clasp, your knit tube needs to be 1"–1½" (25–38mm) shorter than your desired finished measurement.

How Many Beads Do I Need To Pre-String?

This is the most commonly asked question I get about planning French Knitter jewelry. The number of pre-strung beads required depends on several issues:

* How many pegs will you use?
* How often will you add a bead?
* How long do you wish to make your piece?

As you work on projects in this booklet, you will become familiar with the process and be able to predict the requirements. Try this approach to the issue: Place at least 20–40 beads on the fiber of choice, choose the number of pegs you want to use, and knit about a 1"–3" (25–75mm) tube. Remove the head from the main body (your stitches will stay in place) and determine the number of beads per inch. Multiply this number by the finished length and you'll have the number of beads to string. I always add about 10 more beads. This approach allows you to see your work in progress.

Tip: As you are pre-stringing the beads, place a Wonder Clip at the beginning and every 100 beads thereafter. This way you can keep track of how many beads you have strung.

Common Jewelry Lengths (finished)

Choker	16" (405mm)
Princess	18"–20" (470–510mm)
Matinee	23"–27" (585–685mm)
Opera	35"–37" (890–950mm)
Women's Bracelet	7" (180mm)
Men's Bracelet	9" (230mm)
Anklet	10" (255mm)

Project One:
Basic Bracelet

DESIGNED BY CAROL C. PORTER

This is a very good project for learning the French knitting method. I will take you through the process from beginning to end with written instructions and step-by-step illustrations. Ribbon is a nice fiber to start with, because it does not have a ply and will not split. Beads are pre-strung randomly, so no special planning is necessary.

Carol Porter

MATERIALS LIST
❖ ¹⁄₁₆" (2mm) polyester metallic ribbon
❖ 2 crimp-end caps
❖ 2 jump rings
❖ 1 toggle clasp
❖ Clear quick-drying glue
❖ Assorted beads and iridescent sequins

Tip: Using the long slender needle threader is easy for two reasons:

1. You can pick up lots of beads.

2. The threader is wide enough to accommodate all fibers.

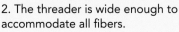

Tip: Wonder Clips are placed at the 100 count of beads. This helps to easily see how many beads are strung and ready to go.

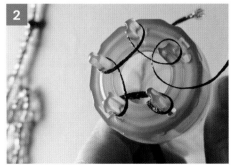

Instructions

1 Get started. Pre-string ribbon with 250 beads. Attach the 5-peg head. Choose a method and stitch. I used Method B (ribbon in front of peg) single stitch (knit over one row).

2 Insert the ribbon. Start as per instructions for Method B Single Stitch (p. 5). Insert the ribbon through the center hole; hang on to the end and wrap the pegs in order.

3 Make a knit stitch. Bring the ribbon to the front of the peg. Use the hook and lift the first loop up, over, and off the peg… this is a knit stitch.

4 Knit the first three rows. Knit the first three rows with no beads; then add one bead between each peg, every row. Note: If you plan to use a closure finding on your bracelet, the first three and last three rows of just knitting with no beads allows space for the closure to be attached.

5 Knit to length. The wrist measurement for this bracelet is 7" (180mm). When the tube measures 6½" (165mm) long, it is time to stop knitting. To find the length: Measure from the base of the pegs to the end of the tube.

6 Cut the tail. Cut about a 15" (380mm) tail of ribbon. Note: I ended up using only 200 beads by the time I reached 6½" (165mm).

7 Complete the knitting. Knit three rows without beads; then cast-off.

8 Begin to cast off. Make the stitch.

9 Continue to cast off. Pull the ribbon end out.

10 Tie off. Make a knot in the end, pulling it very close to the tube. Add a small amount of clear, quick-drying glue to the knot with a toothpick.

11 Add the end cap. Set the end into the end cap and clamp one half, then the other half. Trim off ribbon tail.

12 Open the ring. Open jump ring using a twisting motion.

13 Complete the bracelet. Insert the jump ring in the end cap eyelet, insert one of the closure findings, then twist the jump ring back to close the ring. Repeat Steps 11–13 for other side.

Tip: When the tube grows to approximately 1½"–2" (40–50mm), you can always remove the main body from the head to check on your work. If you are not happy with how things look, remove the stitches from the pegs and pull. All the knitting will come out, but the beads will remain on the ribbon.

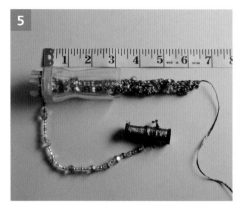

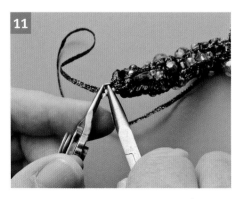

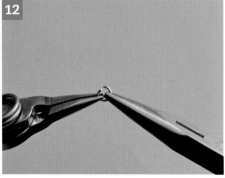

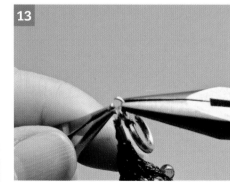

Silver & Black Necklace & Bracelet

DESIGNED BY CAROL C. PORTER

Rachel Porter

This project uses two different fibers to create an attractive result. The addition of a pendant gives this necklace a strikingly different look. You can include a bracelet to complete this ensemble.

MATERIALS LIST

❖ Assorted sizes and shapes of black, silver, and clear beads for both pieces

Necklace
❖ Yarn with metallic threads
❖ Clear monofilament .012" (.30mm)
❖ 1 pendant with bail
❖ 1 set ribbon clamps
❖ 2 jump rings
❖ 1 lobster claw clasp

Bracelet
❖ Black stretchy cord .05mm
❖ 1 toggle clasp
❖ 2 crimp beads

Instructions

For Necklace:

› Length: 21" (535mm)
› 6-peg head
› Method B (Yarn and monofilament in front of peg) single stitch

1 Pre-string the beads. Pre-string the monofilament only with 234 assorted beads.

2 Knit the first 7". For Rows 1–60 or approximately 7" (180mm), knit with yarn and monofilament together using Method B single stitch.

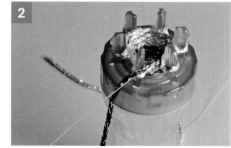

3 Row 61. On the next row, cut a 6" (150mm) tail from the yarn.

4 Cast off yarn. Cast off yarn only as you continue knitting with the monofilament.

5 Hide the tail. Use a darning needle and thread the tail down through the center of the tube and out. Twisting the main body off from the head will make hiding the tail much easier. Remove needle, but do not cut excess yet.

6 Knit with monofilament. The following rows are knit with the monofilament only using Method A (wrapping each peg). Drop one bead between every peg every row until all beads are knit (approximately 39 rounds).

7 Continue with the tail. Before next row: Thread a darning needle and insert the yarn through the center of the core and out through the beads; remove the needle.

8 Knit with both fibers. Pick up and knit with both the monofilament and the yarn to the front of the peg (Method B) as you did at the start. Knit 60 rows or the same length as the first side; cast off.

9 Weave in ends. Thread a darning needle and weave yarn ends into knit tube; cut off excess.

10 Knot the ends. Make a knot in the ends as close to the tube as possible. Feed ends down into the tube, bring needle out, and trim the excess.

11 Attach the clasps. Apply a small amount of glue to the end of the tube and attach the ribbon clasp at each end.

12 Attach jump rings. Attach jump rings and lobster claw clasp following instructions for Basic Bracelet (p. 7).

13 Attach pendant. Carefully open the bail and attach the pendant to the necklace; close bail.

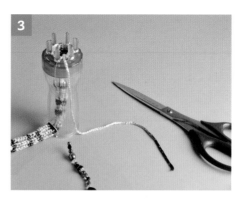
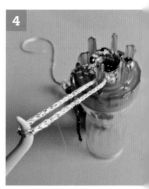

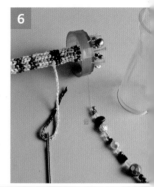
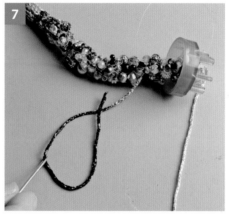

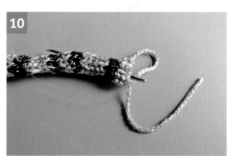

For Bracelet:

› 5-peg head
› Method B
  single stitch

1 Pre-string the beads. Pre-string the black stretchy cord with 200 beads.

2 Knit the bracelet. Place a bead between every peg, every row until all beads are used—approximately 6" (150mm) un-stretched.

3 Attach the closure. Attach toggle closure as for the Basic Bracelet (p. 7).

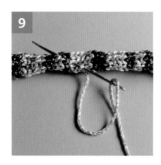

Project Three:
Date Night Clutch, Earrings & Bracelet
DESIGNED BY CAROL C. PORTER

Add sparkle to your favorite clutch by making a French-knit handle. Create earrings and a bracelet to match, and you are on your way to making memories…and oh so sophisticated!

MATERIALS LIST
❖ Assorted white and clear beads and iridescent sequins for all pieces

Clutch Handle
❖ Satin silver bead stringing wire .012 (.30mm)
❖ 1 set rectangular rings (can use D-rings or O-rings)
❖ 26-gauge wire

Earrings
❖ 2-ply silver lamé cord
❖ Earring wires
❖ 4 crimp beads

Bracelet
❖ Clear stretchy cord
❖ 2 crimp beads
❖ 1 toggle clasp

Rachel Porter

Instructions

For Handle
› Length: 12" (305mm)
› 5-peg head
› Method B (Monofilament in front of peg) single stitch

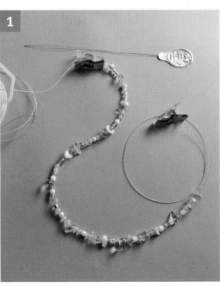

1 Knit. Pre-string bead stringing wire with 460 assorted beads and sequins. Begin knitting, adding one bead between each peg on every row.

2 Attach to clutch. Wire to clutch at the rectangular rings. The first attachment is using the .012" (.30mm) stringing wire and a touch of glue at the base of the tube.

3 Reinforce connection. String 26-gauge stringing wire through some of the end beads and over the rectangular ring; do several wraps around the wires to create a lead to the handle.

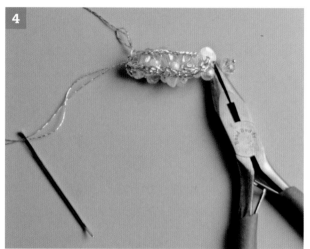

For Earrings:

> 4-peg head
> Method A (Wrap all pegs)
  double stitch

1 Knit. Pre-string 2-ply silver cord with 40 assorted beads and sequins. Knit all rows, adding one bead between each peg every row.

2 Add the drop bead. Thread a crimp bead; then add the drop bead.

3 Continue threading. Bring the cord back through the crimp bead.

4 Complete the drop bead. Using a darning needle, feed the end of the cord up through the knitted tube and out the other end. Crimp bead with pliers.

5 Attach the earring wires. Thread both ends through a crimp bead and an earring wire; then bring them back through the crimp bead. Crimp bead with pliers. Feed ends into the tube to hide. A small dot of clear-drying glue just below the crimped bead will help secure it. Trim ends. Repeat Steps 1–4 for second earring.

For Bracelet

> 5½" (140mm) (un-stretched, not including toggle clasp)
> 5-peg head
> Method B single stitch

1 Pre-string the beads. Pre-string clear stretchy cord with 210 assorted beads and sequins.

2 Knit. Begin knitting. On all rows, add one bead between each peg every row.

3 Attach toggle clasp. Thread end through crimp bead and toggle eyelet, then back through crimp bead. Crimp bead with pliers. Add a drop of clear-drying glue just below the crimped bead and hide the end down the center of the bracelet. This is the same technique as for the earrings. Repeat for other half of the closure.

Headbands for Girls

DESIGNED BY CAROL C. PORTER

Create a darling headband for special occasions or add some sparkle to a princess hairdo. It's off to the party you go…makes a great birthday gift as well. You are knitting a tube so it easily slips over an existing headband.

MATERIALS LIST

✤ Girl's size headband (fabric covered is ideal)
✤ Variegated perle cotton
✤ Assorted shapes and sizes of white, clear, mauve, pink, purple, and green beads and iridescent sequins OR assorted buttons

Rachel Porter

Tip: To avoid shifting, take some extra stitches along the inside edges of the headband.

Instructions

For Headband:

› 6-peg head
› Method B (Perle cotton in front of peg) single stitch

1 Pre-string the beads. Pre-string perle cotton with 300 beads. Note: This amount of beads fits over a girl's size headband.

2 Knit. Add a bead between pegs 1, 2, and 3 only, on every row. This allows for the beads to sit on top of the headband while the back will be flat against the head.

3 Attach to headband. After casting off, open the tube at both ends. Slide onto the headband, adjust for evenness, and sew ends onto the headband.

Bohemian-Style Headband, Bracelet & Necklace

DESIGNED BY CAROL C. PORTER

Matthew Porter

What goes out of style almost always comes back...much like leather headbands and spool knitters. Truly never out of style, th combination of leather and beads makes a statement that is both comfortable and stylish. The leathe you choose needs to be fairly pliable for easiest stitching. A tricky knotting system makes the bracele adjustable! Using irregular rock chips with uniform beads gives this necklace a wonderful, natural look

MATERIALS LIST

Headband
- Deerskin leather lace
- 9 pony beads

Bracelet
- Deerskin leather lace
- 4 pony beads

Necklace
- Brown variegated perle cotton
- 68 EACH of agate, turquoise, and amb glass irregular beads
- 68 EACH of copper, brass, and turquois round beads
- 2 turquoise pony beads (optional)
- 1 peace symbol pendant

Instructions

For Headband

> 4-peg head
> Method B (Leather in front of peg) single stitch

1 Begin knitting. Measure a 12" (305mm) tail; then, begin knitting. Knit rows 1–5.

2 Row 6. On Row 6, place one bead between pegs 1 and 2 only.

3 Continue. Repeat Steps 1 and 2 until all 9 beads have been knit.

4 Complete knitting. Knit last 5 rows; then, cast off.

5 Cut the tail. Cut a 12" (305mm) tail. The tails are used for tying the headband.

Tip: Because you need to keep track of the number of rows, mark the first peg with a permanent marker or touch of fingernail polish.

or Bracelet

4-peg head
Method B (leather in front of peg)
single stitch

Begin knitting. Measure a 6" (305mm)
; then, begin knitting. Knit Rows 1–3.

Row 4. Knit Row 4, placing a single
ad between pegs 1 and 2.

Row 5. Knit as usual.

Row 6. Repeat Step 2.

5 Rows 7 and 8. Knit as usual.

6 Row 9. Repeat Step 2.

7 Continue. Repeat Steps 3 and 4.

8 Complete knitting. Knit the last 3 rows.

9 Cast off. Cast off and leave a
6" (150mm) tail.

10 Tie the knot. To make the adjustable knot, or Chinese sliding knot, I tied
the black (left knot) onto the white; then
the white (right side knot) onto the black.
I tightened the black knot, then the
white one.

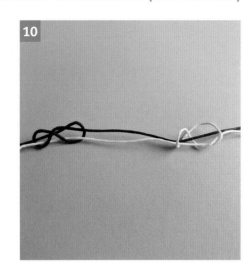

or Necklace:

Length: 21" (535mm) length
5-peg head
Method B (Perle cotton in front
of peg) single and double stitch

Pre-string the beads. Pre-string all
beads on the perle cotton. Note: This
cklace has a set pattern. The beads
ed to be strung in this order: 3 round
ads; 3 irregular beads; repeat, keeping
colors in the same order.

Rows 1–3. Knit Rows 1–3 using Method
single stitch.

Rows 4–6. Knit Rows 4–6 using Method
double stitch.

Row 7. Knit Row 7 with double stitch,
cing one bead between every other
g (after 1, 3, and 5).

Row 8. Knit Row 8, placing one bead
tween every other peg (after 2, 4, and 6).

Knit all the beads. Repeat Steps 4 and
ntil all the beads are knit in.

The last 6 rows. Do 3 rows of double
tch and 3 rows of single stitch; cast off.
te: If you desire a longer necklace, knit
re rows at the beginning and end of the
cklace. Shorten by knitting fewer rows.

Optional: Pony beads. Place a pony
ad at the beginning and end of
e necklace.

Attach findings. Tie a knot as close to
ch end of the tube as possible; apply a
all amount of glue to the knot. Attach
mshell end cap, ring, and lobster
w clasp.

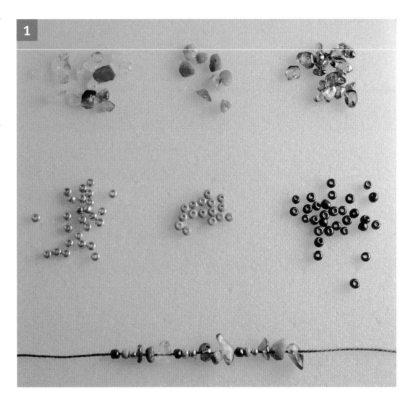

Up-for-the-Date Victorian Necklace & Bracelet

DESIGNED BY ALICIA CARR

This necklace has a Victorian look with rich colors. It can be worn long or doubled for a two-tiered matinee length. Alicia crafted the brooch using six buttons from her collection; if you like the look, find some metal buttons and add them to the necklace. Alicia cleverly uses an extra heart button as a feature on the bracelet in the clasp area.

Matthew Porter

MATERIALS LIST

Necklace
* Red-violet/lavender/ purple variegated rayon floss
* Assorted amber, gold, yellow, and red-violet 6/0 beads

Optional Brooch
* 6 assorted brass buttons
* 1 pin back

Bracelet
* Red-violet/lavender/ purple variegated rayon floss
* 2 crimp beads
* 2 jump rings
* 1 lobster claw clasp
* 1 brass heart button
* Assorted amber, gold, yellow, and red-violet 6/0 beads

Instructions

For Necklace:

› Length: Single strand 48" (1220mm), doubled 24" (610mm)
› 4-peg head
› Method B (Floss to the front of the peg) single stitch

1 Pre-string the beads. Pre-string 1008 of the assorted beads onto the rayon floss.

2 Knit. Place 2 beads between every other peg every round until all beads are used; cast off. Note: The 4-peg head has enough space to allow for placing 2 beads between the pegs. This is a nice design option with a very different look.

3 When making a long necklace, there is no need for a closure finding. Join by weaving the two ends together. Tie a surgeon's knot and cover the knot with a dot of glue. Hide the ends down in the center of the necklace and trim the excess.

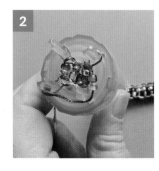

Optional Brooch

Using a string to help, arrange 6 brass buttons together in a cluster and glue in place. Attach a pin back with glue.

For Bracelet:

› Length: 7" (180mm)
› 6-peg head
› Method B single stitch

1 Pre-string the beads. Pre-string 288 of the assorted beads.

2 Knit. Add 2 beads between every other peg every round (as you did for the necklace); cast off.

3 Finish up. Follow Steps 10–13 for the Basic Bracelet (p. 7). Add a heart button into the jump ring if desired.

utterfly Necklace & Bracelet

SIGNED BY ALICIA CARR

nning color
mbination,
emovable
terfly pendant,
l easy-to-wear
gth makes
s necklace a
versation piece.

ATERIAL LIST

ssorted turquoise
nd gold beads for
oth pieces

cklace
litter thread
lonofilament
crimp beads
ing and lobster
aw clasp
jump rings

celet
litter thread
lonofilament
head pin (or
ringing wire)

Rachel Porter

Instructions

For Necklace:
› Length: 20" (510mm)
› 5-peg head
› Method B single stitch

1 Pre-string the beads. Pre-string 785 assorted beads onto the glitter thread and monofilament together. Note: For this project, Alicia found the glitter thread often broke during knitting, but did not want to give up the color and texture the thread added. By incorporating the monofilament, she reinforced her knitting and kept the thread from breaking.

2 Knit. Add a bead between each peg on every row until you reach your desired length. The 785 beads will give you a 20" (510mm) necklace.

3 Attach lobster claw clasp. Thread end through crimp bead and jump ring, then back through crimp bead. Crimp bead with pliers. Add a drop of clear-drying glue just below the crimped bead and hide the end down the center of the necklace. Twist open jump ring, insert lobster claw clasp, and twist jump ring closed.

4 Attach pendant. The butterfly is a purchased pendant with a hole in the wing. To make this a removable pin, Alicia glued a gold bead over the hole and hot glued a pin back to the back of the butterfly. The necklace can be worn with or without the pendant (pin), and the pin can be placed anywhere you choose on the necklace.

For Bracelet:
› Length: 9½" (240mm)
› 5-peg head
› Method B single stitch

1 Pre-string the beads. Pre-string 385 assorted beads onto the glitter thread and monofilament together.

2 Knit. Add a bead between each peg on every round.

3 Tie off. Join the bracelet by weaving both ends together. Tie off using a surgeon's knot, and add a small amount of clear, quick-drying glue to the knot with a toothpick.

4 Attach dangle. To create the bead dangle, use a strong bead stringing wire and string beads as shown. Attach the dangle to the bracelet by running the wire through the bracelet and back down through the beads. Cut off excess wire.

Madonna Necklace

DESIGNED BY ALICIA CARR

This necklace is simple, elegant, and can be naughty or nice! The small gold and silver beads nestle in with the 8mm pearls and knit with monofilament makes this necklace look like the beads are just floating. The silver-trimmed, mother-of-pearl inlay cross is the perfect pendant to finish this piece. It's amazingly simple to make!

MATERIALS LIST

- Monofilament
- 800 assorted 6/0 silver and gold beads, and 8mm pearls
- 1 cross pendant
- 1 bail

Rachel Porter

Instructions

For Necklace:

- Length: 23" (585mm)
- 5-peg head
- Method B single stitch

1 Pre-string the beads. Pre-string the 800 assorted beads and pearls in a random order.

2 Knit. Add a bead between every peg on every round. I love the look the pearls mixed in with the gold and silver beads creates.

3 Tie off. Close the necklace by weaving the ends together. Tie off using a surgeon's knot, and add a small amount of clear, quick-drying glue to the knot with a toothpick.

4 Attach pendant. Carefully open the bail, and attach the pendant to the necklace. Secure the bail into the stitches.